Annie's Adventures

Fulton Books, Inc.
Meadville, PA

Published by Fulton Books 2021

ISBN 978-1-64952-329-7 (paperback)
ISBN 978-1-64952-330-3 (digital)

Printed in the United States of America

Annie's Adventures

Annie Learns to Ride a Roller Coaster

A.G. Prout

Today Mommy and Annie had plans to go to a fair. Annie had never been to a fair and was very excited to go. There would be lots of walking, so she had to wear the proper shoes. She had to wear the right clothes because it was warm outside. She helped Mommy pack a lunch with some of her favorite snacks. Then they hit the road.

Once they arrived, Annie saw all the big rides, and she felt butterflies in her tummy. As she walked through the front gate, all the sounds and colors and people made her feel not so nervous. Everyone was laughing and happy.

Annie saw the bouncy house and got in line.
Mommy was too big, so she could not go in with
her, but she could see Mommy standing just outside
the ride. It helped her feel more like having fun.
She bounced and laughed.

Annie tried a few more rides like the Ladybug Circle and Hoppin' Frog Swing. Mommy stood and waved, watching her as she was having fun. Some of the rides made Annie's tummy tickle, and that made her laugh. Her next ride was the biggest yet: the roller coaster.

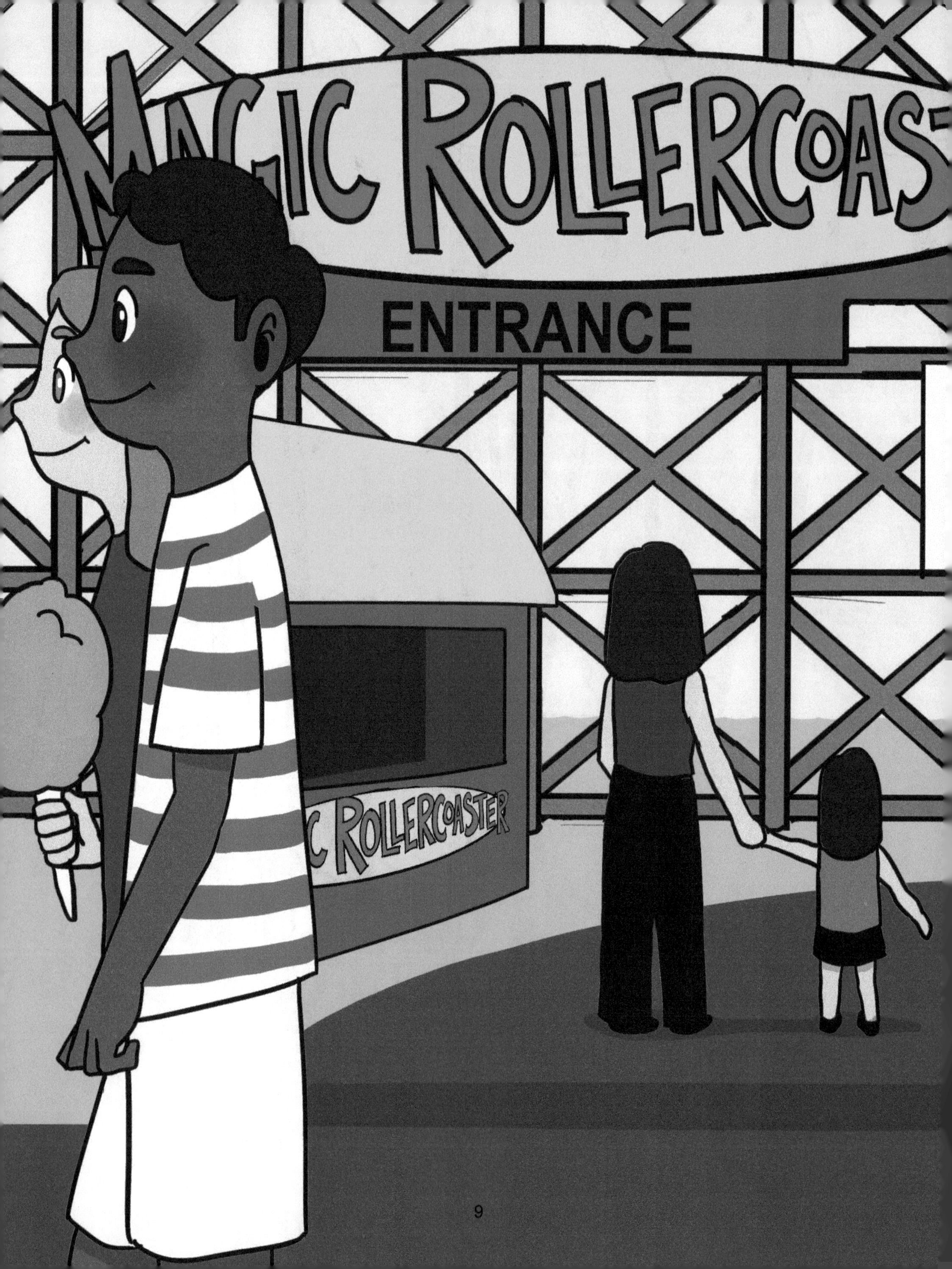
MAGIC ROLLERCOAS
ENTRANCE
C ROLLERCOASTER

As Mommy and Annie got in line for the roller coaster, Annie was very relieved to see that Mommy could ride with her. Annie watched the roller coaster go fast by her while she stood in line. Annie was starting to feel those butterflies again and held Mommy's hand tight. Her mom hugged her and told her how brave she was being, and Annie thought of the other rides she had ridden and then started to feel excited to ride the roller coaster. Just then it was time to get on the roller coaster.

Annie listened to the safety workers' instructions then saw them give a thumbs-up. She felt the roller coaster move, and she held her breath. She felt Mommy put her arm around her as she held on tight to the bar in front of her. The roller coaster went faster and faster. When it took its first turn, Annie's tummy did a little flip, and it tickled her. She let out a laugh she could not stop.

The roller coaster went faster as it went down the hill, making her tummy really tickle, and she laughed and screamed with surprise as the roller coaster turned then went up and down small hills. Sooner than she thought, the roller coaster slowed down and came to a stop. Annie was sad to get off the roller coaster. She had loved it.

Annie's mommy asked her if she liked the roller coaster. "I loved it and want to do it again!" Annie replied. So back in line they went. Annie never got tired of going on the roller coaster and even started raising one hand on the hills like Mommy did. That made it super fun; she felt like she was flying.

By the end of the day, she had ridden a lot of rides, so Annie was very tired. She loved the bouncy ones, the swirly ones, and the swings, but she especially loved the roller coaster. While riding home in the car, she fell asleep feeling her tummy tickle, and it made her smile from the inside. She now knew that those butterflies that she sometimes felt were good. They meant she was about to have fun.

About the Author

A.G. Prout was inspired to create Annie by interactions with her daughter as a young child. She and her daughter have had many adventures and have had to work together to develop trust. It takes understanding and patience to reach past the word "no" we often get from children. This book hopes to inspire children to find their way past "no" and to be brave with the support of their families.

CPSIA information can be obtained
at www.ICGtesting.com
Printed in the USA
LVHW061929160121
676686LV00013B/723